Life Lessons
I Learned in the Milking Pen

Bob Lively

TREATY OAK PUBLISHERS

Publisher's Note

This is a work of personal memoir. All characters, events, and locations are based on the author's family and his experience. Any resemblance to other persons, living or dead, is purely coincidence and unintentional

Copyright © 2021 by Bob Lively
Cover design by Kim Greyer
All rights reserved.

No part of this book may be reproduced, scanned, or distributed in any printed or electronic form without permission from the author. Please do not participate in or encourage piracy of copyrighted materials in violation of the author's rights. Purchase only authorized editions.

Printed and published in the United States of America

Treaty Oak Publishers

ISBN-978-1-943658-81-7

DEDICATION

In loving memory of my parents:
Mary Alice Keeton Lively
and
Henry McKee Lively

Foreword

When you get old, many things become clearer. This reality is certainly true, at least in my case, as I have pondered the sources of my beliefs and values which have guided me throughout my life. And to be sure, my parent's guidance was a powerful influence on me, and a very good one, but so were the experiences brothers and I shared when we were children.

As this good book written by my brother will attest, we little guys spent time with Granddaddy on his farm in East Texas, which influenced the kinds of men we would become. And although these learned life lessons were subtle in their delivery at the time, they nonetheless shaped our views on the value of all human beings, regardless of the color of their skin, their level of education, or the world's perception of their success.

Being with Granddaddy in the field, the barn, or the milking pen was a privilege none of us could fully appreciate until later in life. We were aware of his genuine kindness, something he practiced daily, and his view on the promise of the next generation we represented. But we failed to understand how these qualities distinguished him amidst the rural poverty and racially bigoted setting in which he lived, neither of which defeated his perception of what was right and good.

As we can now see, the life lessons Granddaddy taught us were unintentional. It was not his words, but how he lived, that demonstrated what he believed and conveyed to us. In fact, his responses to our unending questions were often brief, almost to the extent that we sometimes thought them incomplete. However, upon reflection, we now better understand the meaning of his responses and he was consistent: Be kind to all people. Be generous in sharing what you may have that they do not. Don't be influenced by the noise around you. Always remember that you represent your family's character in all that you say and do.

Bob's book is a thoughtful reflection of some of the more memorable experiences we shared with our granddaddy, episodes in life which were meaningful at the time and more so today.

William H. Lively

Introduction

My paternal granddaddy, William Jesse Lively, was born in 1898 in an unpainted shack located near the community of Augusta, Texas. That commuunity was tucked so deep into the piney woods of East Texas that no railroad ever saw a reason to lay steel near its tepid pulse, and no highway crew was ever instructed to connect it to anything resembling significance.

Even into my adult years, the single road leading into Augusta remained a primitive, red-dirt trace that penetrated a thick pine forest and was marked by washouts and defined by deep ruts capable of ripping the muffler off a brand new Chevrolet. By the time my granddaddy entered this world as the youngest of the twelve children born to William Henry Lively and Mary Penick Lively, Augusta was already half-dead, and for the whole of his eighty-two years, it would continue to suffer a slow, ignominious demise.

Today, all that remains is a cemetery and three historical markers erected by the State of

Texas commemorating an attack by local Indians in the years just prior to the fall of the Alamo.

When I was a boy, Granddaddy would carry me and my older brother Bill to Augusta to fish for bluegills in nearby Pedro Creek, and on each of those sojourns into his hometown, he would slow his 1950 Chevrolet to a complete stop adjacent to those historical markers and crank down the car's dusty window. Then he would read aloud what we already knew: a few of our ancestors, none of whom were named Lively, had been attacked and slain by a band of local Indians for reasons long lost to history.

Every time I read the story of that slaughter, I felt always conflicted. On the one hand, I was, of course, troubled by any tale involving the killing of people, and most especially people I was told were kin, but on the other hand, I felt a deep sense of pride in knowing that my three brothers and I were sixth-generation Texans.

And it seems, such pride is at the same time every Texan's birthright and far too often an impediment to being understood, much less accepted, by non-Texans the world over.

But even as a boy born into the post-Civil War cotton tenant farmer class, my granddaddy was proud of being a Texan. No doubt, his life was defined by the drudgery of stoop labor. From the age of six, he worked in the planting and harvest seasons from sunup 'til dark. Any creature comforts he enjoyed were both primitive and minimal, at best, and what few pleasures existed for him consisted of cane pole fishing on a stock tank or red squirrel hunting in autumn.

To describe his existence as "difficult" is to understate the obvious: My granddaddy was born into a system that relegated poor white people, along with most rural Black Texans, to the rank of slave. These folks labored for a white landowner, or, if you will, for "the man," for wages barely sufficient to keep a family clothed and fed. "The man" provided the shack.

Granddaddy's primary respite from the drudgery was a one-room school located somewhere near Augusta and a Primitive Baptist Church where he somehow learned the Gospel without assuming the burden of the mental disorder known as any form of religious fundamentalism. His education consisted of only eight grades, because he dropped out early in the ninth grade when a teacher threatened to whip him for some breach of the rules. He enjoyed telling how he slipped out of the schoolhouse's front door without being detected and mounted his horse to gallop all the way into his future.

I've long suspected he recognized that both his station in life and a pre-determined, not to mention, bleak destiny required no more than eight years of education. He abandoned that school knowing how to read and write, and how to count, add, and subtract. For one so limited by the harsh circumstances far beyond his control, I suppose he figured eight years to be sufficient.

However, his decision to quit school would play a pivotal role in my life several decades later, a story I will share later in the body of this book.

The question that has intrigued me for a good part of my life concerned the etiology of this man's acquisition of uncommon, and at times even close to, mystical wisdom. I've long marveled at the breadth and depth of this man's wisdom while remaining puzzled as to both its origin and its simple profundity.

And, of course this question always confronted me with the larger question about the source of all wisdom in general. How does it happen that some of us are wise, and, therefore follow a steady course of living meaningful lives, while others of us seem to get knocked around for a lifetime like a steel ball in a pinball machine?

Does wisdom emanate from formal education in general, and/or from reading in particular? Or, is it derived from our life experience, or in the common parlance of the current culture from the so-called "School of Hard Knocks?"

Is it bequeathed to us by our family of origin in much the same way we "inherit" our genetic composition? Or, is its origin a more mysterious Source.

During my decade tenure as a pastor in a large Presbyterian church in Dallas, I once decided to take a break from the stress and the daily grind of that position and embark on a road trip. My exact destination was unclear, except for the desire to visit once more "the land of enchantment," or New Mexico. After a two-day drive, I ended up on a highway bearing signs inviting the traveler to explore a national historic site known as "Chaco Canyon."

As good fortune had it, I accepted the invitation and turned off the highway and onto a road about as rough as any I'd ever traveled. At its terminus twenty miles later, I happened upon the ruins of what had once been a magnificent city and home to a sizeable population of the Anasazi, or "ancient ones."

The people who inhabited this city lived at least a thousand years ago. As I would later learn, they were the first of their kind in the American Southwest to abandon the cliffs and the caves of the nearby canyons to build their houses, their religious sites, and their common buildings on the plains separating the canyon walls.

As I walked a few miles amid the ruins, I marveled at the remarkable feats of engineering made evident in the perfect ninety-degree angles of the corners of their buildings and in the geometrical complexity of their ancient construction. This was no mere village, but was rather an expansive city comprised of freestanding buildings, roads leading to trade routes, and irrigation canals. These intertwined waterways were designed so artfully as to create an ancient masterpiece of both engineering and architecture.

The more I studied the ruins of Chaco Canyon, the more I wondered how any people who had no access to information regarding standard engineering principles could construct such magnificence so long ago. And this question remained with me until very recently when I happened upon a documentary about the ancient ones of Chaco Canyon.

In this video production a university professor of archeology inquired of a young native descendant of the Anasazi how his ancestors could have built their city in Chaco Canyon. The young man offered the professor what I read to be a knowing smile, then said,, "They had help."

"Help?" The professor's raised eyebrows revealed his incredulity. "Help from whom?"

"Help from the Spirit," the young man said, holding his smile like it was a secret. The professor was likely a bit thrown off his script by this sudden and unexpected, not to mention unscientific, reference to mysticism. Nevertheless, the young descendant of the Chaco Canyon people smiled like a man in possession of a truth the rest of the world could little understand, much less accept.

And in that young man's answer to the interviewer's question, I at last discovered a satisfactory answer to my own question regarding the Source of all true wisdom. It comes not from us, but rather originates in a place or, if you will, in a Person, much, much higher than ourselves.

And there was my answer and my solution to

a question concerning my granddaddy that had weighed on me for years. It had been there right before me for all along, but I had failed to see it.

Right away I questioned the cause of my blindness. Was it because I didn't see my granddaddy as a particularly religious man? Or, was it because I failed to see him as a deeply spiritual soul, a man spent his life working the land as he lived on a steady combination of hope and backbreaking labor with horse-drawn farm equipment more suited to the nineteenth century than the twentieth.

The more I thought about it, the more I decided that any human being who by vocation becomes wholly dependent upon the elements for survival draws inevitably and inexorably close to the Spirit we call God.

I don't recall Granddaddy as being a particularly religious man in the sense of being regular in his church attendance, although he did attend church on occasion and even assumed the role of an adult Sunday School teacher in his later years. But, in retrospect I do now see he was a deeply spiritual man who worked the sandy loam of East Texas and, no doubt, paused regularly from his plowing behind one of his big horses to gaze into the sky and to ask for help.

And I further believe that over the years and more than seven decades of working the land and praying in his own kind of unique, highly personal manner, he entered into a profound and intimate relationship with the Holy Spirit. This bond blessed him not only with decent amounts of rain and sunshine, but also with the gift of a rare wisdom that transcends education and is far superior to what most folks call common sense.

In reflecting upon my unique and subjective experience with his wisdom, I can now see that every lesson he taught me in the simplest of terms was always grounded in love. I understand that it was not so much a love that came from him but one that came through him.

And in his generosity, he passed it on to me and to his other grandchildren. And as I entered my three years of the study of Scripture in a theological seminary, I saw that it was the same love Jesus expressed in everything he did. It was that power which transformed a Jew named Saul from a fire-breathing sociopath into a saint, and ultimately, and arguably, into the inventor of Christianity.

Moreover it was the love that guided me through my school years and into a most challenging college experience, and then into the three glorious years in seminary that led to close to a half century of meaningful ministry.

To judge any fellow human being by following a mere cursory assessment is to miss the essence and the complexity of that person. For if I've learned anything at all in my years of training to be a pastoral counselor, it is that every human being is more complex than we can possibly imagine at first glance.

I once was told by one of my mentors, this one a psychiatrist, that the human personality is more complex than even the human anatomy. Experience has taught me that such an observation is incontrovertible. We are, all of us, complex beings, and such was certainly true of my granddaddy. To glance at him would be to believe he was one more unfortunate, uneducated, and simple peasant, who had toiled under a broiling Texas sun for a lifetime to achieve nothing more than survival.

But, in truth, he was far more than met the casual eye or the cursory glance. He was a highly intelligent man, a voracious reader. He devoured every National Geographic magazine that arrived in his mailbox each month, and he not only comprehended what he read, but he retained the information with the memory of a scholar.

Throughout his long life, he developed and maintained a fierce sense of moral rectitude that drove his every decision. Long before I had come to know him, he had dedicated himself to the discipline of doing right instead of merely discussing righteousness. As a consequence, he was a man who could be trusted, and even more important, was trusted by those who knew him.

If he had any vices, I never saw them. I never heard him use even one swear word, or drink anything containing spirits, or shirk a chore demanding attention, or punish anyone for anything.

His kindness was so consistent and so reflexive as to make me believe that quality was his foremost expression of faith.

His sense of humor was legendary in both his end of the county and, of course, within his family. He loved to laugh, and he would slap one knee after hearing some story or observation that hit him just right. But his laughter was never a response to anything derisive or belittling, because he chose to build people up rather than employing humor to tear them down.

Perhaps his greatest gift was storytelling. When I would join him on the front porch once the summer evening dishes were done, he would tell me and my brothers stories about the old days in the piney woods. He would join his father and some of his neighbors to hunt black bears or track a cougar that had enjoyed feeding on some neighbor's livestock.

As mesmerizing as those tales were, his best stories were about the numerous ghosts who inhabited the woods and the creek bottoms nearby. On more than one night during my childhood, I lay awake for hours in a back bedroom, worrying about those ghosts and wondering just how safe I was beneath layer upon layer of my grandmother's homemade quilts.

His love for his family was palpable, and his influence on me and his other grandchildren was invariably a blessing. Not all of the lessons he shared with me were given in the milking pen, but the first and most important one definitely was.

I was much too young and far too inexperienced to comprehend its meaning at the time, but during the decades I've lived and toiled in the challenging profession of pastoral ministry, it has served me well ,both as a guide and as an anchor. It steadied me in a world and in a church where the disorder of narcissism is far more common than any expression of true, selfless piety.

And in the remainder of this book, I will list the lessons he taught me, most of which were given as an example without the need for any kind of explanation or justification.

My granddaddy, as a generous and as loving a man as anyone could ever meet very simply showed me how to live. And I will be forever grateful to him for his willingness to share his most important life lessons.

As I enter into the closing chapters of my own life, I feel compelled to share some of his wisdom with you, dear reader. The prayer, which serves as the predicate for this book, is that this book both honors the memory of my granddaddy and proves beneficial to every reader.

Lesson 1

The Three-Legged Stool

Granddaddy's milking pen was barbed wire enclosure of probably no more than four hundred square feet located in what he called "the lot." Some farmers know it as "barn lot," but for my granddaddy it was very simply "the lot," and it was a space he would frequent twice a day for the whole of the thirty-two years I was blessed to know him.

Come cloudburst, sleet, snow, or broiling summer sun, Granddaddy ambled to the lot, and entered the milking pen every morning at four-thirty and then return again at five every afternoon. Whether morning or afternoon, his cows were always present and bawling at the gate courtesy of his two devoted cow dogs, Poncho and Nellie.

Both dogs recognized the requirements of their commitment and would roll out of their beds beneath the house each morning and then race into the darkness beyond the woods until they reached a distant pasture where they summoned the cows in need of milking to begin their desultory trek toward the pen.

They performed the same duty every afternoon. What amazed me the most was their dedication to carry out this chore without being asked. They seemed to know what was expected of them, and they always performed magnificently. And even before I reached the age of ten, I had come to believe that Poncho and Nellie were more trustworthy than most people.

The barn was a wooden building constructed in 1890 of enormous, rough-hewn logs and plank siding. It was composed of two horse stalls, a loft where bales of coastal Bermuda hay were stored, and where perhaps as many as a dozen wooden boxes were located throughout. Hay filled the boxes to serve as nests for the laying hens.

The ground surrounding the barn was carpeted in discarded corn shucks and desiccated corncobs that long ago had been pecked clean by several generations of chickens. The barn's only protection from the brutal East Texas sun and the occasional life-giving showers was a corrugated tin roof that was blanketed in rust long before I was born.

Sometimes when a gentle rain visited, I climbed into the hayloft and savored the soothing sounds of the passing shower as it drummed a steady cadence against the tin above my head. With nothing but a hay bale to serve as my pillow, I reclined in that old loft and dreamed about what I might do with the decades of life that seemed to spread before me like a vast uncharted ocean. It provided a wonderful place to mix dreams with prayers and blur the boundary between the two. And for a boy with nothing more to offer God than a vivid imagination, it was a safe, and even secret, place to listen and imagine the rain sharing glimpses of challenges and wonderful opportunities that awaited me.

But as much as I loved to hide from the world in that old loft, I learned to listen for wisdom in the milking pen.

Once Granddaddy reached the gate of the milking pen, he launched into instructions for his cows as one by one he permitted them entrance. When four or five were inside, he closed the gate and then lifted an old bucket from a wooden peg in a three-sided shed.

Next, he carried the bucket to the first cow to be milked. Flipping the bucket upside down, he sat on it like it was a stool. Before he ever touched the cow he spoke to the animal in a strange dialect.

"Saw," he said.

This, I deduced early on was a command for remaining still. If the cow did not comply, he repeated the command in a gruffer tone. What always amazed me is that his cows seemed to understand the command and most often obeyed by remaining still until the milking was done.

But on the rare occasion that some old cow chose to move around a bit, Granddaddy reverted to English and said, "Don't you step on me, cow!"

I suppose over the course of his own childhood, he had learned to use the word "saw." From my perspective, this single word seemed to be sufficient to accomplish his purpose of keeping order in the milking pen.

As a young boy, I always felt honored when he lifted two old buckets off the wooden peg in the cow shed, because it meant I was invited to sit right next to him as he milked. If my presence troubled the cows, they never demonstrated impatience or resentment. The bucket right next to Granddaddy's was the seat of honor and, even more, the locus for the possible receipt of wisdom.

On one particular summer afternoon in my pre-teenage years, my granddaddy ceased his milking long enough to turn to me and say, "You know, Bobby, nobody can ever sit on a two-legged stool. It must have three legs or it will fall over every time."

I had no idea as to the meaning in this observation, and neither did I understand why he chose to share it with me in such a mundane moment. Nevertheless, I hung on to it and pondered its possible application for nearly two decades before at last I discovered the answer to this apparent riddle deep within the stacks of a seminary library.

I first attempted to make some practical sense of Granddaddy's three-legged stool in my geometry class during my first year in high school, once our instructor explained that only three points could exist in the same plane. But the more I considered this principle, the more I struggled with how it might illumine Granddaddy's puzzling observation. Giving up, I decided that this particular axiom would shed no light on a possible solution to what Granddaddy meant.

At least I was wise enough not to ask him to explain the meaning in his metaphor. I knew I had no real idea of his meaning, but I was also intuitive enough to know he expected me to discover the truth for myself.

For whatever reason, he seemed to share Freud's notion that "all truth is discovered." So, I never inquired of him the meaning of his observation as I carried the riddle into my four years of undergraduate study at a fine little liberal arts college in North Texas. Nothing I heard or read during those four challenging years "unlocked" the mystery of the three-legged stool.

At long last, I discovered, at least to my own satisfaction, the profundity in my Granddaddy's metaphor.

For in the summer of 1970, I took a course in New Testament Greek where early on I was assigned the task of translating from Greek into English Matthew 22: 37-40. An hour or so into my work, I became far more interested in the message in the text than I did with the actual process of translating the words themselves.

And there it was before me: the truth of my Granddaddy's observation written in ancient

Greek and contained in two commandments given to the world by Jesus Christ.

I viewed the first leg on three-legged stool to be the commandment "to love the Lord God with all of your heart, and with all of your soul, and with all of your mind." And the second Leg, as Jesus put it is "to love your neighbor," while the third is "to love yourself."

Years later as I trained to become a pastoral counselor, I came to see that Jesus's two commandments are the very foundation for our happiness, and indeed for all successful relationships.

Jesus's two great commandments are no secret, and neither was Granddaddy's three-legged stool, of course. But most of us within the church and far beyond the walls of it live our lives as though we have no clue that all true happiness, along with any realistic hope for the gift of genuine inner peace, is inextricably linked to one's love of God. That peace is also tied to one's willingness to love his or her neighbor, as well as to the commitment to love oneself always appropriately.

Jesus' two commandments and Granddaddy's three-legged stool are not at all difficult to comprehend. In truth, they are quite simple concepts that invite us to commit our time and our energy into loving God first and then to follow that commitment with the decision to love our neighbors with the same energy we devote to ourselves.

The problem is not in the comprehension of the concepts. Rather the challenge lies in the willingness to discipline ourselves to live our lives always balanced on the three-legged stool.

In retrospect, I have no doubt that Granddaddy lived a balanced life, despite the hardships that attend a sharecropper's existence. He never escaped the poverty into which he was born, plus he survived the Great Depression before sending both of his sons off to fight fascism. In the face of all that, my granddaddy was a genuinely happy man. He loved his life just as he loved the people in his life.

His relationships among his family and in the world were solid and highly functional, in the sense that he was both admired and trusted.

I spent decades of trial and error before I came first to see and then appreciate the "secret" to his happy and peaceful existence. I don't fully understand all of what made him who he was to me and to his family, but today I do know this: every time I rode to town with him on some kind of errand, I was always proud to be introduced as his grandson. And as far as I was concerned back then, there could be no higher honor, and today after more than seven decades of living, I've never known a higher honor.

Lesson 2

Patience

Rain meant life on the farm. Yet during seven formative years in my childhood, the heavens refused to give up the wet stuff in every corner of the Lone Star State. The city of Dallas even resorted to pumping in brackish water from the Red River to keep its citizenry supplied, and I recall vividly the taste of salt in our water during the miserably hot seasons that separated one school year from the next.

The city seemed to cope and make do, but on the farm, the wells threatened to dry up, while the cash crops died an agonizing death in the unrelenting drought. Day after tortuous day the radio weatherman proclaimed what we already knew: no rain was in the seven-day forecast.

But all of that changed one memorable summer night in the mid-fifties. My sweet grandmother and I sat together on the front porch shelling what purple hull peas had survived the brutality of that summer.

Poncho, the cow dog, was the first to sniff what I hoped just might be a coming miracle, as a bank of clouds slowly climbed above Mr. Henderson's withered corn stalks just beyond a red-dirt road older than the State of Texas.

Poncho lifted his head and whimpered as though warning us not to hope. Nellie's refusal to abandon her comfortable nap was proof enough that dogs likely know more about sudden changes in barometric pressure than the rest of us.

Content to study the dogs for clues, I continued my commitment to the purple hulls. But Grandmother rose to her feet to search the hope now quickly forming in the southern sky.

"Well what do you know? It looks like it could rain... at last."

She gave such emphasis to her final words, I feared her frustration might jinx the arrival of this apparent miracle. I quit my work to stand and to join Grandmother in studying the sky.

A loud clap of thunder seemed to awaken the entire world. The cows waiting their turn at the milking pen gate ceased their bawling, and even the hens nesting in the nearby garage hushed their complaints as the songbirds followed their example.

All of a sudden, the earth fell silent, as if awaiting instructions. Lightning flashed and thunder answered. And that's when we spotted it.

Rain drops fell with such fury on Mr. Henderson's corn patch, the dead stalks danced. The fresh rain was so close, we could inhale its fragrance, and yet, the moisture refused to cross the road. Dark clouds hugged the distant horizon forcing the rain to fall from a clear sky.

"The Devil must be beating his wife," Grandmother said as she resorted to folklore to explain the phenomenon of rain falling from a clear sky.

I nodded at her quaint observation while hoping that Lucifer might cross to our side of the road to beat the old gal over our farm. But all such thoughts proved fruitless on that summer evening of long ago as our hope dried up, only to stir up a cloud red dust.

Soon thereafter I presented my conundrum to Granddaddy in the milking pen. I wanted an answer to the obvious injustice of rain.

"How could rain fall on Mr. Henderson's dead corn and miss our parched land completely?" My demanding tone revealed my frustration.

Never stopping from his milking to consider my question, Granddaddy turned to me. "Son, it's like this: 'it rains on the just and on the unjust,' and one of these days it will rain on us."

He punctuated his rhyme with a grin, signaling he was done with his commentary on the issue of any kind of fairness in the ways of nature.

Only later, much later did I discover that his response was rooted in Scripture in that the first part of his observation was a rough paraphrase of Jesus' teaching as it is contained in Matthew 5:45b:

"For he (God) sends rain on the righteous and on the unrighteous."

By the time I discovered that his wisdom was rooted in Scripture, I was a young, eager seminary student astonished to acknowledge that my "semi-literate" granddaddy was in fact a student of the Holy Bible. And I suspect what I respected the most about him was the humility that tempered his knowledge.

He never preached to us, nor attempted to win an argument through "proof texting," which is to prove a point by selecting a biblical text as the proof of his own particular point of view.

In the retrospect granted by more than half a century, I can now see that his study of Scripture was a private matter to him, one which required nothing in the way of either exhibition or presentation.

He was not one to wear his religion upon his sleeve, but rather he was a quiet and inconspicuous man who lived his life according to what he believed was the Word of Almighty God.

Of course, his response was not nearly so much about rain as it was about the spiritual gift that is patience. He had been richly blessed with that particular gift, and in his own gentle way, he was inviting me to embrace it and to make it my own.

What I most appreciated about that moment was the fact that he didn't scold me or diminish me in any way. He simply invited me to be patient, because issuing invitations was yet another simple expression of his gift for patience offered to a grandson who, like many people, would struggle for a lifetime with impatience.

Lesson 3

Love Is Patient

Granddaddy owned precious few prized possessions. Among them was an old fiddle, an antique 22. Caliber bolt-action rifle which very seldom missed its target, and a short fiberglass fishing rod which served him well in the creeks and stock tanks in and around Houston County, Texas.

In the late spring and summer months he enjoyed taking his grandsons fishing on either Silver Creek or Pedro Creek, where, if fortune shined, we'd catch a few bluegills and perhaps a catfish or two. It was always a great adventure to set out for a secret fishing hole we figured was likely unknown to the rest of the world. He never failed to assist us in baiting our hooks and waited until we launched them into the water before he began his own artful work with his miniature fiberglass rod.

On one particular summer evening, I was done with my fishing early, packed up my gear in a hurry, and ran back to the car to win the coveted prize of sitting in the old Chevrolet's front seat with the window rolled down all the way home. My brother Bill had enjoyed this place of prominence and comfort on the way to the creek, and I was determined it was to be mine for the remainder of our adventure.

I arrived at the empty car before either my brother or Granddaddy realized I had abandoned the creek bank. I swung open the old car's back door and tossed my rod and my tackle box on the floor of the back seat.

As I slammed the rear door shut, I realized to my horror that Granddaddy's little fiberglass rod had been resting against the car and had fallen partway into the back seat with its tip stuck in that narrow space separating the door's hinges from the car's frame.

Unable to move, I stood staring at the severed rod with most of it now lying in the red dirt next to my feet.

A profound sense of panic washed over my entire being as Granddaddy and my brother walked toward me, with Bill balancing his rod upon his shoulder like a soldier. I had no idea that Granddaddy hadn't carried his prized fiberglass rod it down to the creek bank like he always did. Nevertheless, I knew I had just destroyed his beloved fishing rod and I was required to confess it all to a man I not only respected, but even more, revered.

As Granddaddy and Bill drew closer, I searched for just the right words to convey both the exact details of my mistake and also words sturdy enough to convey the depth of my heartfelt regret.

At first, I stammered, like I always do when I get nervous, but I managed to blurt out, "Granddaddy, I slammed the door on your rod and broke it into two parts. It's ruined."

I then squeezed my eyes shut before promising him I would save up my allowance for however long it took to buy him a new one out of the Sears catalog. As I opened my tear-filled eyes, I looked up to see him smiling at me.

He placed his hand upon my shoulder and said, "Son, I wish you hadn't done that."

On the long ride home I sat next to him in the front seat with the window rolled down and with the first cool breezes of the summer evening washing against my anguished face. He had to be more than a little disappointed and, perhaps even angry, but he said nothing further about the entire incident. He drove into the coming darkness nonstop toward another one of Grandmother's sumptuous country suppers, replete with three different kinds of homemade pie for dessert.

He never spoke another word to me regarding my mistake. He didn't scold me, or shame me, or belittle me in any way. There was absolutely no tension between us. And, as far as he was concerned, no unresolved issue lingered between us.

Decades later, as a seminary student whenever I heard a professor speak of grace, I would smile in the acknowledgment that I knew very well of the reality of which they spoke, because I had experienced it long ago near a creekbank deep in the piney woods of Houston County, Texas.

Lesson 3b

*I*n the spring of my first year of high school, I traveled to my grandparents' farm with my father.

I always enjoyed my alone time with him and most especially when I rode with him to the farm. The deeper we traveled into the pine and hardwood forests of Houston County, the more stories he shared with me about growing up as the dirt-poor son of a tenant farming family during "the Great Depression."

I suspect the stories never came easy for him, because for the whole of his life, he had done his best to cope with his rough childhood by repressing as many memories as he could. Nevertheless, every so often he remembered a story from his difficult past and shared it without any particular expectations regarding sympathy or even empathy.

For him, his early past was a fount of raw recollections of the suffering caused by being trapped in a system that treated him and his family like slaves, while promising no future other than a life of stooped labor and the cruelty of grinding poverty.

But on this particular day that hangs in my memory like a puffy summer cloud, Dad pulled his car to the shoulder of the road and stopped still several miles from the farm. Of course, I was puzzled, but before I could inquire as to the meaning underlying this surprise stop, my father pointed to a large open pasture surrounded by a loblolly pine and hardwood tree forest. Fenced in rusty barbed wire, this field was home to perhaps no more than a half dozen young pine saplings, no taller than knee high to a grown mule.

Still pointing, my father said, "One year during the depression and between the harvest and planting seasons, your granddaddy single-handedly cleared this field of all of its trees by using nothing more than an axe."

He then said, "Can you imagine?"

And because I'd never been called upon to face such an enormous challenge, I couldn't, of course. Somewhat staggered by even imagining the immensity of it all, I said, "How long did it take him?"

"A full month from sunup to sundown every day, including Sundays."

"How much did he earn for this job?" I pushed.

My father sighed, thus signaling either incredulity or a profound sadness. "Oh, probably about thirty dollars, I suppose."

And once more I could not imagine anything so awful as having to remove a big chunk of a forest from its sandy moorings in only one month's time and for only thirty bucks. Because I could think of nothing else to say, I asked one last question. "How did he do it?"

Dad smiled. "Oh, one tree at a time, I suppose. But you know Granddaddy. He was never one to quit what he began, and he could always be counted on to finish. Because that's who he was."

And over the course of my long career in the pastoral ministry, each time I faced a challenge so difficult that I considered quitting, I would reflect upon a verdant cow pasture in the north end of Houston County, Texas, where long ago my granddaddy chose to keep his promise and stay at a close-to-impossible job to the very finish.

Lesson 4

The Blessing of Perspective

In retrospect, my freshman year in college was the toughest year of my entire life. I was in no way equipped academically for the high-octane school I chose to attend.

To be clear, all the deficits in my preparation were of my own creation, save for the fact that I'm just not all that smart. As a result, once I arrived on campus and met my new classmates, I realized I was in way over my head.

I found myself surrounded by kids my own age who were not only gifted intellectually, but also determined to do whatever was required to pursue careers in medicine, law, ministry, or higher education. While I'd been a strong student in high school, even being named to the National Honor Society, I arrived on that small college campus convinced I didn't belong.

The truth was, I was no more than an average student with nothing to bring to the effort but a mind that was extraordinary only in its abject ordinariness. Furthermore, I had no idea what

I might do with my life. While I'd considered the ministry as a career, I was certain I did not possess the intellectual gifts required to pursue a career that involved three years of seminary beyond the four years of undergraduate work.

After I bombed my first biology exam, I decided I would do whatever was required to make certain I would never fail another exam, much less a full course. And from that day forward, I studied like I'd never studied before, so much and with such intensity that I denied myself any social life whatsoever.

By Thanksgiving of that year, I had turned my fortune around through hard work and finished the first semester with decent grades, but also with the growing awareness that I didn't belong in this place.

The social life on this campus was predicated upon the Greek system, a social constellation I would come to abhor due to its pettiness and its often cruel patterns of excluding folks who were a bit different and, like me, socially awkward. In February of that year I was invited to join a fraternity judged by many to be coolest of all, and I made the mistake of pledging the thing.

As a result, I spent the spring of that miserable year being hazed and harassed by the active members, several of whom impressed me as sadists. Through it all, I studied and continued to enjoy a modicum of academic success, all the while struggling with the burgeoning awareness that I did not belong at this place and, even more, I did not belong in any fraternity, much less in the one I had chosen to join.

At last, May arrived, and I was released from the bondage of near-constant study to return home to the family who loved me and who believed in me, even when I found it impossible to believe in myself. Much to my astonishment, I completed that year with good, but certainly not spectacular, grades. That summer I found a job unloading boxcars at a big warehouse in the industrial section of Dallas.

For eight long hours every day, I stacked crates of groceries on pallets and/or wrangled 500-pound barrels of linseed oil with a primitive tool called a barrel jack, only to be paid two dollars and seventy cents an hour. The management hung a thermometer in the boxcars we were unloading, along with instructions to abandon those cars once the temperature reached one hundred and twenty degrees.

Several times that summer, in fact almost every day, the temperature came within a few degrees of compelling us to escape, but it never did reach or exceed one hundred and twenty degrees. Nevertheless, the heat in those boxcars was so intense and so protracted that for the whole of that summer, I labored precariously close to the bounds of my own physical and psychological endurance.

The summer I had so anticipated and counted

on to be a respite from the stress of academia had become a nightmare. What happened next was likely far more a Freudian trick than any kind of conscious decision on my part.

After a particularly miserable mid-August afternoon with the temperature pushing well above one hundred degrees, I made the mistake of leaving a two-dollar crowbar in the boxcar I had raced to unload before quitting time. Unbeknownst to me, an engine picked up that particular car that night and had hauled it off to somewhere else, along with the crowbar I'd dropped on its metal floor.

Early the next morning, the warehouse boss met me on the loading dock to inform me they didn't need me anymore. I was being blamed for the lost crowbar, and in his mind, such was a unforgivable offense. As a result, I was fired.

I'd never been fired before and in fact I'd never before even imagined I could be fired. I'd worked hard for that warehouse in inhumane conditions, and every day that summer I had come home filthy and exhausted, not to mention both physically and even emotionally depleted.

The most difficult part of that morning was calling my mother and asking her to come pick me up. I felt both ashamed and gloriously happy as I waited for her to come take me home from this purgatory I had called a job for the past three months. Sitting on that dock for the last time, I watched my fellow workers trudge into the boxcars to begin their eight-hour ordeal of burning up while lifting heavy boxes and crates and stacking them neatly on a wooden pallet. I felt for those unfortunate men, while I thanked a loving God that my days in those boxcars were forever done.

On the long drive home, my mother inquired, of course, as to the exact cause of my termination. I told her of the lost crowbar, but as was typical of her, she perceived a far more realistic rationale:

"Oh, I suspect they're down-sizing due to the fact that school is but two weeks away," she said.

I was grateful for her interpretation because her version removed the stigma of failure and its attendant shame.

At dinner that evening, my father chuckled in the wake of the crowbar story before informing me that tomorrow he planned to take me to a Chevrolet dealership to buy me my very first car with my summer earnings, along with a large supplemental gift on his part. True to his word, of course, the very next morning we drove to a local dealership, where within a half-hour, we purchased a brand new 1965 turquoise Chevrolet Corvair, the same car the famous consumer advocate Ralph Nader would later proclaim to be "unsafe at any speed."

The total cost of that little car was exactly $2,080, and my earnings paid for less than half of that amount. But still, I was the owner of a brand new car, which the college would allow me to keep and to drive because I had with some degree of success navigated the turbulent whitewater rapids of my freshman year.

My sophomore year began much as my freshman year had ended. I returned to the library, where I pored over my textbooks and wrote countless papers for a western civilization course called "Basic Studies," and my course in sophomore English. Unlike my freshman year, my grades were good to the point of encouraging me to believe that, in spite of my all-too-obvious intellectual limitations, I was in fact learning how to learn.

What minor success I experienced buoyed my self-confidence to the point where I no longer viewed myself as a source of shame to my family and/or to the many people back home who had expressed confidence in me and who had assured me that I would surely do well, no matter what career I chose to pursue. That autumn was for the most part a season marked by one minor success after another. I permitted myself the luxury of dating some, and I even attended a dance where I enjoyed myself immensely.

On the surface, my life appeared good and on track. I was in a cool fraternity, I was making better grades, and most important, I was making and enjoying new friends, but deep inside, I knew there was something wrong with my soul or with my spirit or however one might wish to describe it.

In moments of honesty I admitted I was still emotionally exhausted from the stress of the previous year and also from the hell that had been my summer in the boxcars.

In retrospect, I now can see that I should have gotten help, but at that point I was much too naïve and uninformed to recognize I was seriously depressed to the point of needing medical attention. Consequently, I pushed on all the while making good grades and pretending I was enjoying my new life as a "cool fraternity guy."

A terrible anxiety had so captured my soul and contaminated my thoughts that the best I could manage was to find some modicum of solace in the library. I continued to pore over textbooks, memorizing what I was not capable of comprehending and writing endless papers on subjects in which I had no interest whatsoever. In order to cope, I ate alone in the huge campus dining hall each evening and then hurried to my car. Then I would drive out into the rural countryside to watch a local farmer feed his livestock.

Frequently, I drove the little car onto a soft shoulder of a gravel road and stepped out long enough to watch a man dressed in faded overalls, the exact color of Granddaddy's, setting out hay bales and cubes for his cattle. And in that always-poignant moment, I found myself envying that farmer without, of course, knowing anything about his personal circumstances.

For all I knew, he could have been up to his neck in debt and/or stuck in a miserable marriage, or so addicted to alcohol or some other drug as to make his life a personal hell.

But the way I idealized only the apparent, this man was living a peaceful and healthy existence, raising cattle and crops without the stress of living in a library. He didn't have to read what I considered esoterica, stuff I was pretty certain I could get along just fine without ever knowing.

After each such foray into the countryside, I would return to the library and remain there until it closed. Mine was a lonely existence driven by a terrible fear of failure and defined by, at best, a pseudo interest in doing something worthwhile with my life. I didn't know it, but I was trapped in a classic double-bind.

On the one hand, I was terrified of failing and thereby disappointing my parents who had sacrificed so much to see to it that I could attend such an excellent little liberal arts college, while on the other hand, I hated what was required of me to prepare for a future about which I had no clue and, in truth, zero passion. I had no idea, whatsoever, regarding what I wanted to do with my life other than the hard-earned decision never again to labor on a warehouse dock.

But other than that, I drew a blank every time I attempted to consider a career path. In addition, I was much too uninformed either to trust

Providence or to rely upon grace to guide me. I didn't know grace even existed, much less was available for the asking. All I knew to do was to trust myself, to work until I had exhausted myself, and then to work some more.

Everything seemed to come to a head one morning when I awoke even before the sun had risen. In the dark I shambled over to the student union building, where I found the dining room doors still locked. I sat on some stairs and waited until a cafeteria worker opened the dining hall.

After downing a quick breakfast, I exited the building and considered heading toward the library. But I realized it, too, would be closed for the next couple of hours. I turned to find my car parked against a curb, where it seemed to summon me, in silence and mystery, to drive as far away from this campus as I could get in what time was still available to me before the library opened.

I had no plan except to escape as I heeded the car's summons, and within mere minutes I found myself on state highway 75 heading south toward Dallas. But I knew I could not show up at our house unannounced. I would scare my mother and worry my father, so I drove through Dallas and headed southeast toward my grandparents' farm in Houston County.

I realized my sudden appearance might cause them some consternation, but I convinced myself that my visit would be an unexpected and joy-filled gift to them. After all, they were always glad to see me, and by the time I reached the Trinity River in Navarro County, there was no turning back.

I was at the point of no return.

As expected, my grandparents were surprised, in fact, stunned, to see me, but right away their surprise turned to their typical expressions of genuine hospitality. I'd brought nothing with me, an obvious oversight that, no doubt, puzzled them. But instead of inquiring regarding this omission on my part, Granddaddy asked me how long I could stay. They both smiled when I asked if I could spend the night.

And, of course, "Why sure," was the answer offered in near unison.

They invited me in for a late lunch, which was an invitation I was more than glad to accept. As I stepped toward the front porch, both dogs emerged from their beds beneath the house to greet me.

And in that warm and wonderful moment, I felt like I was home for the first time in months.

After lunch, Grandmother retired to the tiny sleeping porch where, as was her habit, she would rest for no more than an hour. After washing the dishes, Granddaddy and I both reclined on the cool linoleum floor in the living room. There we both napped for several moments next to a small electric fan that vibrated with such violence that it appeared to walk across the room.

As I lay there listening to the roar of the last

of the late-summer cicadas in a nearby tree, I thought of school, but just as quickly decided I would only focus on gratitude.

I was grateful to be in that old house Granddaddy and my Uncle Carl had built with their own hands. In that moment I was grateful my grandparents had never owned a telephone. Most of all I was just grateful to be away from that study carrel in the college library and to be with people who loved me.

Before supper, Granddaddy invited me to accompany him to the milking pen, and I accepted. Once inside the pen, he offered me a bucket to flip upside down and use as a stool. I sat next to him as he milked old Blue, an ornery cow who enjoyed terrorizing my younger brother, John.

Without warning, Granddaddy paused in his milking and turned his head toward me. "Son, how is school?"

I hesitated. "Granddaddy, I'm going to quit. I've discovered I'm not what they call 'college material.' I'm not smart enough to go to college, Granddaddy, at least not to this college. I'm not even sure I want to be a college graduate."

That wise old man turned his full body to me. "Son, I sure do wish I'd fallen heir to just a few of your opportunities."

And that was all he said. He didn't shame me. Nor did he scold me. Nor ridicule me in any way.

Out of his deep reservoir of wisdom, he reminded me that, unlike him, I'd been blessed with almost unlimited opportunities to do with my life something far more significant than whining, grousing, and complaining about a little hard work. After an early breakfast, I drove back to school and arrived on campus in time to make my afternoon classes.

Later that semester I was named to the Dean's list, and three-and-one-half years later, I graduated right on schedule. And seventeen years later, that wonderful college named me a distinguished alumnus, an honor I never expected, but have long cherished.

Granddaddy taking a break

Lesson 5

Love Is Kind

A few years ago I was privileged to hear the Dali Lama speak at the University of Texas in Austin. The President of the University introduced him as a man who viewed kindness as his religion.

Right away I was struck by the similarities between this holy man and world leader and my granddaddy, a man who had spent the majority of his life stuck in the cruel tenant farmer system. From conversations with Granddaddy, I learned he was a fervent believer in the Lordship of Jesus Christ, and as an avid reader and student of Scripture he made kindness his foremost religious expression.

Without question, Granddaddy was always kind to his family, and he was just as consistent in his kindness to neighbors, and even to his farm animals. Whenever he drove the six miles in either direction between his farm and the very small town of Grapeland, Texas, he always stopped and offered a ride to any person walking on the shoulder of the narrow farm-to-market road, regardless of their race or gender.

As was the rigid rule of the piney woods culture, the Black travelers always sat in the back seat, while all white travelers felt free to join Granddaddy in the front. Despite who might become his passenger, Granddaddy always managed to find something to talk about. He loved visiting with his riders and in some cases catching up on the latest news within the county.

While he was kind, he did not always want to be accommodating.

The only house visible from his front porch was the home of his neighbors, Mr. and Mrs. Henderson. For whatever reason, Mr. Henderson never owned any kind of vehicle, at least not in the 32 years I was given to share time with Granddaddy. Most every time he and I set out for town, with both of us in the front seat, Granddaddy mumbled his hope that he didn't have to carry Mr. Henderson to town.

Granddaddy's driveway was a good hundred yards of ruts, which was a distance that offered Mr. Henderson ample time to view us attempting to make a furtive drive to town. And as we rolled at a slow pace down those ruts, Granddaddy repeated over and over again as he mumbled, "I don't want to take that old man to town."

Almost as predictable as sunrise, by the time the front tires reached the red dirt road, Mr. Henderson had popped out of his front door like the little bird in a cuckoo clock and yelled. And without exception, Granddaddy hit the brakes and waited for Mr. Henderson to make his slow descent down a sizeable hill until he reached the car. Granddaddy welcomed him like he was a long-lost personal relation.

I surrendered my place in the front seat in deference to my elder, and Mr. Henderson and Granddaddy carried on an animated conversation all the way to town and then again on the return trip.

And through it all, even when he had to delay his return trip due to the slow pace with which Mr. Henderson often ran his errands, Granddaddy was always kind and patient with a man who had by circumstances, likely beyond his control, come to rely upon my Granddaddy for all of his transportation needs to and from a town not even big enough to be the county seat.

The valuable lesson I learned from Granddaddy's relationship with Mr. Henderson was this: It is all-too-human not to want to be kind in every situation, but kindness is always the right decision, no matter what one might feel at any particular time regarding any particular set of circumstances. Kindness is always the right decision, and that is so because kindness is an expression of the divinity that dwells within every human soul. Every time we choose not to express it, we fail to connect to the God within us.

Soon after I began writing my column in the *Austin American-Statesman*, a man phoned me one morning to convey two pieces of information:

One, he appreciated the column and, two, he grew up with my father in Houston County and was a distant cousin, whose last name was Lively.

He asked if he might come see me, and I offered an immediate invitation. He appeared at my office the very next morning, right on schedule, and pumped my hand as he displayed what I imagined was a trademark grin that had likely served him well throughout his life.

Once he accepted the cup of coffee I offered, we both relaxed a bit as we shared the amenities that are the requisites for any budding friendship. When a comfortable pause afforded me the opportunity to probe, I asked him to tell me about himself.

He appeared more than pleased with my invitation as he told me about his combat experience in France during the Second World War. And that's when his eyes brightened as he described his trip home in what he called a 'troop ship.' He claimed he had no idea where exactly he would be discharged, but he knew that the very minute Uncle Sam cut him loose, he would head home to Houston County.

That is when he astonished me by saying that he planned to make his first stop at my grandparents' house. He called them Uncle Will and Aint Ruby. And he claimed he was close to desperate to savor once more some of Aint Ruby's fried chicken, scratch cornbread, and homemade pies.

The monikers he assigned to my grandparents

didn't surprise me at all because for the whole of life I'd heard them referred to as Uncle Will and Aint Ruby, but what didn't surprise me at all was his familiarity with and fondness for my grandmother's legendary cooking.

Throughout the countless times I visited my grandparents, I witnessed members of our extended family and neighbors turn into the deep red ruts of the farm's driveway. Without exception, each time a visitor's old truck or car rolled toward the house, Granddaddy peered out of a window in the front door and said, "Oh, we don't want company tonight. No, we don't want anyone to interrupt our visit with our grandsons."

Grandmother, who was practically deaf, said, "Who is it, Will?"

Invariably Granddaddy mumbled, "I don't know," before shrugging his shoulders and thus signaling that he had not yet identified them.

Following that he grumbled, "But we don't want company tonight."

However, once his uninvited guests exited their old vehicle and stepped into the yard, the two dogs greeted them. Granddaddy turned into the epitome of so-called "southern hospitality." He always greeted his unwanted guests with the same vigorous shout of recognition. With a wide wave of his arms, Granddaddy hollered, "Get out, get out, and come in. You're just in time for dinner."

And after Grandmother had time to pull back

the window shade long enough to identify her dinner guests, she stepped back into the kitchen to heat pans of vegetables picked from her garden that very day. She re-heated the fried chicken in a propane oven old enough to be declared an antique.

And, of course, she removed what remained of her three different kinds of pies from the pie safe and placed them on a counter in full view of her guests.

Then the old game commenced: the uninvited guests protested and insisted they didn't drop by unannounced to partake of Aint Ruby's legendary cooking when everyone in the room, including both dogs, knew they had. But the more my grandparents insisted, the closer the visitors inched toward those pies and the fragrance of fried chicken warming in the oven.

Within minutes, those protesting guests were seated at the table devouring one of the best country suppers in the whole of Houston County, Texas.

When I was much too young to understand the depths to which kindness must sometimes plumb, and the enormous effort kindness sometimes requires, I questioned my grandparents' sincerity. But as I matured, I came to understand that there was nothing insincere about them.

In what I can only describe as a kind of radical expression of hospitality, they pushed through their negative feelings to insure that kindness was present in their home. And for as long as I knew them, kindness did always prevail both in their home and even more in their souls

I SUPPOSE I WITNESSED one of the most poignant, and memorable demonstrations of kindness on the farm during the week of Spring Break during my final year of college. While other students throughout the country were headed to the closest beaches or to Mexico or the Caribbean, I chose to spend my week with my grandparents on the farm.

I decided it would be a good place for me to rest and to spend time in the hayloft pondering a future that remained a bit cloudy. Besides, nowhere else on the planet could I enjoy authentic country cooking equal to what my grandmother placed before me three times each day. As a result, a week on the farm helping my grandparents wherever I could seemed a good idea.

On the third memorable day of that visit, I plowed part of a big sand hill behind Granddaddy's big draft horse, Nancy. I even got the hang of how to gee and haw, as that big mare remained patient with me through the ordeal of my learning curve. That evening following a sumptuous dinner, Granddaddy and I washed the dishes before retiring to the front porch where we joined his two gifted dogs in watching the sun set.

That's when Granddaddy surprised me with an announcement regarding a man named Joe who was going to drop by some evening soon to talk about buying some of the calves that were born earlier that spring. No sooner had he finished imparting that bit of information than an ancient pick-up truck, with its full beams burning brightly, turned into the long driveway.

I thought it a bit odd that Granddaddy rose from his chair and stepped inside to turn off the porch light.

The truck was so old and so bruised, it appeared dead-on-arrival. As this man named Joe exited the driver's side, the dogs abandoned the front porch and sprinted toward our visitor and jumped on him, all the while dancing about in frenzied excitement.

With the porch still strangely dark, Granddaddy descended the steps to greet the man with a handshake. I followed my grandfather into the front yard, where I was introduced to a man who seemed to have stepped right off the pages of Steinbeck's *Grapes of Wrath*. He was obese and unshaven. His overalls were so ragged, they might become unhitched at any second.

As this old man gripped my hand, I recognized in an instant that he had most likely spent his life doing the kind of physical labor I had sworn an oath to avoid in the wake of my warehouse experience.

Of course, Granddaddy invited him to join us, and the old man followed us to the porch. It remained in growing darkness as the remnants of the day streaked the western sky with its faint, dying light. And for the next hour, the three of us sat while those two old men discussed everything from the market price for beef to our country's involvement in the Vietnam War.

At last, when the night had descended upon the countryside, the owls hooted, and at least a million tree frogs filled the darkness with their songs, the old man in rags plopped the half-chewed-up remains of a straw hat on his head and bid us both a goodnight as he made his way to his old truck. He and my granddaddy never did once discuss the actual sale of the calves, and neither did Granddaddy ever offer to turn on the porchlight.

Through everything, including that old man's precarious descent down the porch steps, Granddaddy kept that porch as black as pitch. Once the man was gone, Granddaddy went inside and flipped on the light switches and once more bathed the old porch in light, a gesture every moth in Houston County seemed to appreciate.

As we both reclined in separate living room rockers, I asked him why we had visited with that man named Joe in the dark.

Granddaddy chuckled and said, "Son, it's a long story."

"I'd like to hear it, if you don't mind telling me," I said.

Lighting his pipe Granddaddy said, "Well it's like this. Long before you were born, that old man was doing farm work down on the border, and for some reason he got in a fight with another farm worker, who happened to be a Mexican. And he killed that other farm worker. He just up and shot him the man dead. The police down there never even charged him with a crime, but the man's family let him know that they would catch up with him someday wherever he went and they would kill him. So ever since that day, he prefers to remain in the darkness, and, to tell you the truth, I can't blame him none."

Now, St. John proclaims in the preamble of his gospel, "The light shines in the darkness, and the darkness did not overcome it."

Of course, St. John's use of the image of the light illuminating the darkness refers to the power of love to remove all shadows cast by whatever forces of evil operate in this world. And John's proclamation is both eternally and universally true.

And on one memorable night in my youth, I recall my granddaddy expressing kindness by keeping us all in the dark.

Lesson 6

Love in a Pickle Jar

St. Paul was wise to avoid a definition of the great mystery that is love. Instead, he wrote of love's foundational characteristics, proclaiming... "love is patient, love is kind; love is not envious or boastful or arrogant or rude. It does not insist on its own way; it is not irritable or resentful; it does not rejoice in wrongdoing, but rejoices in the truth. It bears all things, believes all things, hopes all things, endures all things...."

Because Paul was the first great theologian of the Christian faith and inarguably a spiritual giant, I have long suspected he was well aware of the truth that the great mystery of love does not originate in the human soul, but rather always in God, and then only flows through us, if, that is, we allow ourselves to express it.

And because it originates in the ultimate mystery of God, it, too, remains a mystery.

This means love cannot be in any way defined, even though throughout the ages people have attempted to do so. But again, St. Paul, in his wisdom, only attempted to list a few of love's key characteristics. And I suppose he did this as a way of instructing the folks in ancient Corinth how it is love might or might not appear in their ordinary, even mundane, daily transactions.

As eloquent and as profound as St. Paul's description is, he makes no mention of a pickle jar. This is quite understandable, because I doubt he had any first-hand experience with love being contained in a pickle jar. But my father and my Granddaddy certainly did.

In the early spring of 1937, my father was named the salutatorian of the graduating class of Grapeland (Texas) High School. As such, he had received letters from various colleges and Texas universities inviting him to apply for admission.

All of this must have felt a bit overwhelming to him because no one in our family had ever pursued a college education. Furthermore, he was aware to a painful degree of the harsh reality that his family did not possess even a smidgeon of the financial resources required to send him to any kind of college.

One of my father's beloved teachers, a man named Mr. Gentry, took it upon himself to drive all the way out to my grandparents' rented farm one evening for the purpose of visiting with my father, and with my grandparents regarding Dad's future.

Mr. Gentry was as blunt as he was succinct in his assessment of my father's situation. To begin, he expressed his opinion that while Dad was plenty talented, he was not adequately prepared to succeed at most of the schools that had invited him to apply for admission. However, Mr. Gentry did offer that, in his view, my father would do quite well at what was then Sam Houston State Teachers College, located in Huntsville, not fifty miles from the farm.

Soon after Mr. Gentry's visit, Dad awoke early one weekend morning to plow a big sand hill where he and Granddaddy planned to plant watermelons. No sooner had Dad arrived at the first turn row than he was surprised to see his father sitting on a stump at the base of the sand hill and waving, thus signaling him to take a break and join him in some kind of conversation.

Dad liberated himself from the reins and ropes attached to the plow. As he ambled toward his father, a man he revered every bit as much as all of his grandchildren would later come to do, my father wondered as to the purpose underlying this sudden summons.

Once he arrived next to Granddaddy's place on the old stump, he waited for further instructions, but Granddaddy only lifted his gaze and smiled before instructing my father to sit next to him on the damp sand.

Again, Dad did as he was told. After he was seated, his father lifted from the wet sand what appeared to be more of a tattered feed sack than any kind of useful burlap bag. Granddaddy turned the bag upside down, and an old pickle jar tumbled to the ground.

In telling me this story, my father would describe Granddaddy's smile as wide as he could possibly make it and his eyes as bright as the rising sun. Granddaddy then turned his attention to the pickle jar and said to my father, "This is yours, son."

Granddaddy then gave him one last instruction before he handed him the jar. This order contained in only two words: "Open it."

My father unscrewed the cap and turned the jar upside down. A thick roll of bills fell to the ground.

Granddaddy said, "Henry, your mom and I have been saving everything we possibly could since the day you were born so you could go to college. And ever since all the banks failed, I've kept our savings in this old jar. I counted it last night and there is a little bit more than five hundred dollars in that jar. I have no idea how much a college costs, but I reckon five hundred dollars will get you started. I'm sorry it ain't more, but this is everything we've been able to save."

Of course, Dad thanked Granddaddy before returning the jar to his safe keeping.

As my father resumed his plowing that morning, he thought of all the ways Granddaddy had worked extra hours during the depression just to earn a little extra. In addition to share-cropping on land owned by someone else, he had taught himself the fine art of cutting hair and had spent every Saturday in town working as a barber. He even once heard of some big cotton farms paying workers to pick cotton out around Abilene, Texas, and he drove a Model-A Ford for twenty hours straight before arriving. He stayed for two weeks before returning with what he was delighted to describe as 'a pocket full of change.'

And when he was not off in West Texas or cutting hair, he hauled dairy products to town to sell to Black people whose entrance into the town grocery stores was prohibited by the local Jim Crow ordinances of the day. And finally, he always made himself available to hire on to clear a pasture, or to dig a well, or do whatever he might to earn an extra dollar or two.

Over the course of the first seventeen years of my father's life, Granddaddy managed to save just a few dollars more than five hundred.

As the spring of 1937 turned to summer, my father prepared himself to leave home for the first time and hitchhike the fifty miles separating Huntsville from the farm his parents rented. No doubt, he packed some kind of bag, probably not much more than a tow sack. But being the self-assured yet selfless person he was, he knew he could not possibly take the money in the pickle jar, simply because it was everything.

Within his first few days on campus, he was hired to work in the college library, a job he kept for the three years and three summers, until he graduated with a degree in music education and a Texas teaching certificate.

St. Paul described love with such eloquence and brilliance to the early believers in ancient Corinth. This apostle to the gentiles never met my granddaddy. If he had, he might have included in his immortal description that sometimes love means giving everything to the one you love so that he or she can have a chance to make it in this old world.

Lesson 7

Loving Kindness

St. Paul's second characteristic of love is kindness, while the ancient prophet Micah takes the expression of love one step higher by proclaiming that what the Lord requires of us is that we not simply be kind, but that we in reality love expressing kindness.

The story that Granddaddy began in the milking pen and concluded on the front porch convinced me that he was not only kind, but also that he in truth loved being kind.

He began the story by claiming that his big draft horse was the first to sense the arrival of an ugly black phenomenon slinking down the old dirt road toward a rendezvous with certain heartache. His big mare pawed the ground and turned her ears toward a sound he could not yet hear. Curiosity compelled him to liberate himself from the plow and in his words, he "eased down the slope of the sand hill."

Leaning on a fence post supporting a few strands of rusty barbed wire, he craned his neck until he finally spotted it: a lawman seated atop a big black horse with a double-barrel shotgun draped across his lap like it was some hand-knitted comforter. A shiny tin badge pinned to his shirt highlighted his sweat-stained khaki uniform. He kept a metal whistle clinched between his teeth with such force, as if afraid it might tumble out of his mouth if he ever yawned or issued a verbal command.

Behind him trudged as many as a dozen Black men wrapped about the ankles in a heavy chain that extended from the first man to the last. Each man was shirtless because of the heat and so caked in the red road dust, their skin gave off the hue of the setting sun through a thin veil of summer clouds.

As this string of tightly bound humanity dragged its way down the dirt road, Granddaddy heard the moans of agony and the various other sounds of suffering. Once this train of misery reached the fence post where Granddaddy leaned, the lawman reined his horse to a full stop and blew hard on his whistle.

This band of miscreants tumbled to the ground, one by one like a line of dominoes. Some lay on their back with their arms over their faces to shield their eyes from the sun. Others lay on their sides and panted like tired hounds who had been forced by cruelty to run much too far and much too fast.

Every man was breathless, and each body bore the scars of a life marked by hardship as they languished in the red dirt, gasping for breath and begging for even a dipper of cool well water.

Only the leader enjoyed sufficient slack in the chain to permit him to sit in some measure of comfort. This man managed to study the young plowman's countenance from his place in the dust as Granddaddy scrutinized the man's orange face. Granddaddy told me he wanted to appear friendly to these men in chains and even to the sadist who sat upon the horse, but he was at a complete loss for words. Soon enough, he decided to limit any interaction between himself and these miserable souls to the first man in line, who was the only man whose face he could observe.

Granddaddy decided a nod would prove safe enough, and no sooner had he completed the gesture than the seated convict returned his nod with a grin. Then he made a request so ridiculous, he must have imagined it would prove impossible. "Hey, mister, play us a fiddle tune."

Now this man covered in red dust could not have known my granddaddy was then regarded as one of the best fiddlers in all of Houston County. In fact, he often was invited to play for house dances or compete in some old fiddler's contest in an adjacent county.

The first time I heard this story, I said to Granddaddy, "What did you do?"

"I went to the house to get my old fiddle, and when I returned, those men were still there in the road like a pack of worn out old dogs. I was a bit timid about playing anything at first, because I didn't want that man on the horse to get riled. But once I spied the man who'd made the request grinning at me, I began fiddling. And once I did, all the men on that chain gang sort of came together and helped each other form a semi-circle in that old road where they all smiled at me as I played. And the second I was done, the lawmen blew his whistle and that chain full of men trudged on to somewhere else. And every single one of those men nodded their appreciation as they passed by where I stood. Once they were out of sight, I carried my fiddle back to the house and got on with my plowing."

I never did ask Granddaddy what tune he played. But considering the desperate circumstances in which the request was made, I suspect he played a sacred hymn. And if I were pressed to come up with exactly what it was, "Amazing Grace" would be an excellent guess.

Lesson 8

Abundant Life

In St. John's Gospel, Jesus tells us he came that we might have life and have it abundantly. I did not appreciate the fullness of this proclamation until I reflected upon one of Granddaddy's lessons in the milking pen, given to me when I was about eight or nine years old.

When I was a boy, I did not, and could not, even begin to comprehend the myriad levels and implications of Scripture, but as I matured, I came to appreciate, if not fully understand, the depth of meaning in Jesus' use of the word "abundance."

I suspect the easiest and most common interpretation of "abundance" is to equate it with the acquisition of wealth. It's unfortunate that this is all too often the interpretation today among American evangelicals. The fastest growing and the largest churches are those that preach what is termed "the Prosperity Gospel."

At its basic interpretation, this perversion of the word "abundance" proclaims that God wants us to be rich in the sense of possessing an abundance of material goods. The theological formula is as twisted as it is simple, and it is this: wealth is a certain sign of God's blessing, so send your preacher your money, especially if he or she happens to be a televangelist, and God will bless you with even more money.

Although this rampant belief happens to be successful, it misses the mark regarding what Jesus meant by abundance. When you come to know Jesus as presented in the four Gospels and by reference in the epistles and the Acts of the Apostles, you are introduced to a man who was not all that concerned with wealth, except as the distinct possibility of it becoming an impediment to one's entrance into the kingdom of heaven.

In simple terms, he was neither attracted to it nor repelled by it. As a result, I find it impossible to believe Jesus was in any way equating abundance with the acquisition and accumulation of wealth or with the possessions it might purchase.

So what is the meaning of abundance here in the 10th chapter of John's Gospel, if it does not refer to wealth?

I discovered the answer in a rather bizarre story Granddaddy told me in the milking pen.

Once he was done milking, he stood up and pointed toward the adjacent hog pasture. "Son, a long time ago, there was a well in that big pasture over there. That old well proved quite handy because I dropped a bucket in it to water the hogs every morning and every evening. Yet, early one morning when I was peering into that old dark well, I discovered a fish swimming on its surface.

And for the life of me, I could not imagine how a fish came to be in that well.

"So every morning for the next week or so, I looked for the fish, but I never did see him again. One evening after I was done with the milking, I carried a long pole over to the well. I had attached to one end an old fishing net. I stirred around in that water for the longest time, but I never did see that fish again. That's when I decided I must've imagined I saw a fish where no fish could possibly be.

"But your daddy, who was a boy at the time, was convinced I really had seen a fish in that well. And so, at night he'd slip over in the hog pasture with a lantern tied to a rope. Once he reached the well, he lowered the lantern deep into the well until the thing almost reached the surface. And sure enough that fish rose to the surface and swam about for a bit in the light.

"And over the years, your daddy and I would drop a lantern on a rope into that well every so often, and almost every time, we'd spot that old fish swimming about all around that well. The poor thing could only swim in circles because that's really all a well is, a deep watery circle.

"Over the years your daddy and I discussed ways to free that poor fish from the well. Several times we tried to net him, but we were never successful. Whoever dropped that poor fish into our well was terribly cruel and likely realized that getting him out of there would be close to impossible. I wanted to net him and then put him in our stock tank where he'd be free to swim about for the longest time and feed on all kinds of food for the rest of his life.

"So finally we gave up trying to catch him and we contented ourselves just watching him swim about in the light of that lantern. Over the next year or so, we decided he was some kind of catfish, most probably a yellow.

"The more we watched him, we discovered something else about him we found disturbing. He was growing in a very strange way. His head was getting bigger, but the rest of him didn't seem to grow at all. Before long, he looked terribly deformed. His head was the size of a full-grown catfish while his body reminded me of a pollywog. It was the strangest thing you ever did see.

"Cruelty caused all of that deformity. That's all it was, just plain old ugly cruelty. No fish belongs in a well, ever. That old misshaped catfish couldn't get enough food to grow right proper in that well, just enough for him to stay alive, but not enough for him to thrive.

"And son, just staying alive ain't living. It's only surviving. And the good Lord means for every creature to do far more than just survive, whether it's a catfish or a human being.

"And one night your daddy and I went out to the well carrying our lantern, and the catfish wasn't there. We looked for him every night for a full week, but he never did show up no more.

So we decided he must've died an early death, forever trapped there in that old well."

Ever since I first reflected on that story as a seminary student, I've come to view "thrive" as synonymous with Jesus' word "abundance" in John's Gospel. Countless times in my counseling practice of over twenty-five years, I met with clients who claimed they were "stuck" in a job or in a relationship, or in a belief system where they viewed thriving as impossible. As time passed, their situation proved so painful that they sought help.

Because I was a pastoral counselor, I many times felt free to reference Holy Scripture as a possible guide to the way out of their dilemma. Quite often I would rely upon Jesus' proclamation that he came that we might have life abundantly.

But what does this mean?

Once again, for me it means that Jesus came so that we might come to realize that we are to thrive, or in other words, to swim about in God's love for a whole lifetime.

Or, as my Granddaddy put it, "Swimming around in circles ain't living, because everyone of us was born to thrive."

Lesson 9

The Farm House

By wisdom a house is built, and by understanding it is established;
By knowledge the rooms are filled with all precious and pleasant riches...
                                    Proverbs 24: 1-4

In the spring of my first year in seminary, the Presbyterian Church required me to travel to Dallas to be tested by a psychologist for fifteen grueling hours. One of the many tests administered to me involved drawing a picture of a house.

In my imagination, I traveled back to my grandparents' farm deep in the piney woods of East Texas where I climbed the sand hill. From the perspective afforded by sitting on the summit of that old hill where Granddaddy had grown so many crops and even a copse of pear trees from seeds to full maturity, in my mind's eye I gazed down upon the farmhouse my Uncle Carl and Granddaddy had built with their own hands back in 1949.

At the moment I chose to draw this house, I was in no way certain why, of all the houses I'd called home over the years, I chose this one small house as the subject of my crude drawing.

Two weeks later I returned to Dallas to be interviewed by this same psychologist, who decided to be cold and intimidating. Among other questions, she asked me about the house I had drawn.

I was quick to inform her that my crude rendering was intended to represent my grandparent's farm house, likely no more than nine hundred square feet and a place I loved to visit, but also a house in which I had never lived.

Of course, I was not at all surprised when she asked me why this particular house was so important to me. Because I'd given this drawing a good bit of thought over the two weeks separating the tests from the actual interview, I was once more quick to answer:

"Doctor, I chose this house because, from the time I was an infant until today, this little house has been for me and for my brothers, and for my cousins, the locus of unconditional love. It has always been a safe place where we knew we were welcome. Even more, it is a place where none of us was ever punished, criticized, or shamed, but rather where grace was palpable.

"We were accepted for who we were and we were built up rather than ridiculed or torn down. All of us always knew what it felt like to be part of a house that appeared to us untouched by the ever-changing whims of the fast-paced world in which we lived."

And had I known Scripture back then, I might have added, "wisdom built this house, and the rooms are filled with all precious and pleasant riches..."

In retrospect, I doubt this learned woman, who seemed only interested in discovering what was wrong with me as opposed to discovering what was right about me, would have understood that love fills a house, no matter how small or how humble it might be, with pleasant and precious riches.

Granddaddy in his going-to-town clothes

Lesson 10

Love Is Eternal

Love never ends...
                              1st Corinthians 13:8...

St. Paul declares to the church in ancient Corinth and, even more to the ages, that love is all that is eternal in this world. Everything else comes to an end, including prophesies, speaking in tongues, and even knowledge, but through everything, love remains so powerful, so enduring, and so amazing in its resilience, that it will not and even cannot end. When everything else is gone, love is all that remains.

I accepted Paul's proclamation regarding the enduring quality of love on faith, until recently when I was blessed to accept it on the basis of what I am convinced was a bit of real evidence. And believe me, this evidence was as surprising as it was mysterious.

Once my father was established as a strong student at Sam Houston State Teacher's College in the late 30's, he picked up his guitar and sang again. He was born with the gift for music, and his tenor voice was clear and strong. In fact, his musical ability was so evident that he was invited to sing on a local Huntsville radio station.

When this invitation was accepted, Dad wrote his parents a letter informing them of his radio debut and inviting them to listen, if, that is, they could locate a neighbor prosperous enough to own a radio and the electricity to run it.

After some bit of research, Granddaddy located a family down the old red road who did possess a small crystal radio. The man claimed it played more static than it did actual music. This neighbor invited my grandparents to come to his house the night my father was scheduled to perform.

The big night arrived at last. Granddaddy milked the cows a little early, and Grandmother had dinner on the table the minute he walked through the back door. They enjoyed the meal together with very little conversation. The dishes were done must faster than usual, and Granddaddy tossed the dish water into a side yard before feeding the two dogs a pan of table scraps.

Within minutes my grandparents were in their old car, bumping and rolling down the red dirt road toward their neighbor's crystal set and a promise of generous hospitality.

When the hour for the performance arrived, the man who owned the radio fiddled with the dials, but got little more than an occasional blast of static. My grandparents leaned as close as they could get to the tiny crystal set, but all they could hear was an occasional muffled voice preceded and then followed by more static. They didn't allow frustration to defeat them, and all of a sudden they heard it.

Their son's distinct and strong voice spoke as clearly as if he shared the room with them. And the static was gracious enough to allow them to listen to what they had waited so eagerly and worked so diligently to hear:

Dad announced that the song he had chosen to sing was "You're the Only Star in My Blue Heaven." He then said he was dedicating this song to his mother.

Recently, my daughter, a single mom, was tucking her eight-year-old son, Henry, in bed for the night, when he surprised her by saying, "Mama, you're the brightest star in my sky."

For me, this is incontrovertible evidence of the veracity of St. Paul's proclamation that "love never ends."

This precious little boy not only shares my father's name, but he also possesses his loving spirit. This is no mere coincidence, but rather an illustration of the incredible durability of love.

We might remain skeptical and disbelieving regarding the remarkable similarity in two separate expressions of love that spanned close to a century, were it not for St. Paul's three words, "love never ends."

But St. Paul knew the truth and dared to proclaim it, and so did my grandson, my father's namesake.

ACKNOWLEDGMENTS

No book can be considered complete without a good editor, and once more, I was blessed with the very best, in Ms. Cynthia Stone. Over the course of my nearly half-century of writing, I've lost count of the number of editors I've had in my twenty-three years as a newspaper columnist and as the author of fourteen books. Some I've chosen, while others were chosen for me. And through everything, I've yet to encounter an editor who possesses the skill of Ms. Stone.

And once more, as I've done four previous times, I've elected to have this small book published by independent publisher, Treaty Oak Publishers, and I have thus avoided altogether the hassle of working with an agent or seeking a publisher on my own. And in working with Treaty Oak, I have been blessed to have Ms. Kim Greyer design the cover of this book. Ms. Greyer, who is a professor of graphic design at Austin Community College, is the gold standard of graphic designers.

In addition, I'm grateful to my brother Jim for providing me with the photo of my grandparents, and also to my brother Bill for writing the

Foreword to this book. All three of my brothers, including John, who died 13 years before the writing of this book, like me benefitted from the extraordinary goodness of both our parents and of our grandparents. And all of us were permitted to be successful in our chosen professions by parents who not only acknowledged, but celebrated, our uniqueness.

Also, I thank my wife, Dr. Mary Lynn Rice-Lively, for her assistance with the technical demands of producing this work. Her patience is testimony of a love which has sustained me over a whole lifetime. And finally, I thank my daughter Sarah Hill for her encouragement and my young grandson for his interest in these stories.

ABOUT THE AUTHOR

Bob Lively is an honorably retired Presbyterian minister living with his wife, Mary Lynn Rice-Lively, a former University of Texas associate dean, on an acre in the Texas Hill Country west of Austin. This is his second novel and his 13th book overall.

For 23 years he wrote a regular column in the *Austin American-Statesman*. He was raised in Dallas and educated in the Dallas public schools, and he is a graduate of Austin College and Austin Presbyterian Theological Seminary, where both schools have named him a distinguished alumnus.

For the past four decades, Bob has served the church as a pastor, community activist, college instructor, seminary lecturer, church schoolteacher, certified pastoral counselor, and retreat leader.

Bob with his grandson, Henry

Made in the USA
Columbia, SC
29 August 2021